T0361498

SH*TSCAPES

jovis

SH*TSCAPES

100 Mistakes in Landscape Architecture

Vladimir Guculak, Paul Bourel

jovis

Contents

An Atlas of Failures   08

Paving   10
#01–10

Drainage   20
#11–17

Access Covers   26
#18–24

Street Furniture   33
#25–39

Trees   47
#40–66

Planting   74
#67–89

Kerbs and Edges   91
#90–100

An Atlas of Failures

As cities worldwide transform to address the urgent climate crisis, our public spaces have become a symbol of change for greener and healthier urban environments. Driven by global, national and regional policies over the past decades, our public realm is set to become a sustainable green and blue infrastructure that offers socially equitable, accessible and ecologically conscious spaces. In recent years, the COVID-19 pandemic renewed our love for the outdoors, re-energising public and private sector efforts, and helping to place our streets, squares, parks and plazas at the centre of sustainable development targets.

In the United Kingdom, such efforts saw the implementation of low-traffic neighbourhoods, green streets programmes, funding for tree planting, government support for sustainable regeneration and obligations for biodiversity net gains[1]. As a result, new developments will prioritise green open spaces and ecological enhancements, helping to contribute to the ambitious national statutory target of 16.5% tree cover by 2050[2].

This momentum, seen in major cities across the globe, inevitably triggers questions around implementation and monitoring. With a public realm often underfunded, forgotten, and sidelined for major infrastructure projects and public buildings, it is crucial to investigate how these aspirational changes will be delivered, built and maintained. Recent statistics by the UK's Forestry Commission show that mortality rates for new trees often reach as high as 50%, with around 30% of urban trees dying within 12 months after being planted[3]. With the UK's allocated parks budget dramatically declining by £100's of millions since the early 2000s[4], it is crucial to understand how these policies will be implemented and what our public spaces will look like in the future.

To help deliver this better future, *Sh*tscapes* takes a pragmatic look at what has been built so far. It offers practical solutions to recurring problems which appear across our cities around the world. Started in 2019 and based on case studies in London, this project surveys 100 common issues and draws universal conclusions meant to assist planners, urban designers, architects, landscape architects and contractors in their endeavours. In other words, the publication is a compendium of failures and mistakes to watch out for during a project's planning, design, construction and maintenance stages.

Aggravated by the advent of the internet and social media, the architecture world is hyper-focused on glossy images and flawlessly built projects. Rarely do we see a building's delivery process or how it stands the test of time. Ironically, the time-based discipline of landscape architecture follows this trend as well. *Sh*tscapes* makes the argument for learning from our failures. This book purposefully showcases a mixture of established and recently built projects to reveal design and construction mistakes and uncover the more subtle imperfections appearing after long-term use.

Unlike buildings and large infrastructure projects, our streets, squares and green spaces are relatively simple to build. Sadly, urban design and landscape architecture publications tend to focus on extraordinary projects, often documented shortly after completion and without a focus on detail, making it hard for students and young professionals to understand how things are built.

To bridge the gap, *Sh*tscapes* covers mostly standard design details, construction and maintenance practices. To this end, the book is structured as a checklist covering the basic elements that typically make up a public space: paving, edges, drainage, furniture, trees and planting. And although not exhaustive, it is intended as a reminder of all the things that could go wrong throughout the life of a project.

We hope to encourage our readers to study their environment and practice their observational skills to expand the *sh*tscapes* library.

This publication intends not to shame or blame an individual or a group. The photography deliberately hides the location and context of each problem to better highlight its universality. Often, a *sh*tscape* illustrates an accumulation of failures over time, attributed to a lack of coordination, attention and continuity between all parties involved. In this book, the source of the problem is trivial compared to the search for solutions, of which there are often many. Should an individual recognise their work, we thank them for contributing to teaching future generations.

About the Authors

Vladimir Guculak and Paul Bourel are both landscape architects and founders of studio gb, based in London, UK, a landscape architecture and design practice centred on the idea that thorough investigation and analysis should always guide how we shape the built environment. The research-led studio is devoted to meticulous observation, mapping, photography and documentation of urban surroundings.

For over a decade, Vladimir and Paul studied our cities' extraordinary complexities, contradictions and constraints with a view to embedding lasting green spaces in our increasingly mineral habitat. This research has resulted in a unique specialisation in patterns of social distancing, green walls, urban tree planting, detailing and sustainable materials. Their work is predicated upon craft, observation, research, engagement and environmentally sustainable solutions to establish unique areas of serenity, resilience and solidarity in an accelerating world.

1 In England, biodiversity net gain (BNG) is mandatory under Schedule 7A of the *Town and Country Planning Act 1990* (as inserted by Schedule 14 of the Environment Act 2021).
2 M. Broadmeadow, 'England Tree Planting Increases for 2022/23', *Forestry Commission Blog* [web blog], 16 June 2023, https://forestrycommission.blog.gov.uk/2023/06/16/, (accessed 7 January 2024).
3 *Carbon Gold, Carbon Gold Highlights Urban Tree Survival Rates* [website], https://www.carbongold.com/carbon-gold-highlights-urban-tree-survival-rates/, (accessed 7 January 2024).
4 K. Martinsson et al., 'Funding for England's parks down £330m a year in real terms since 2010', *The Guardian* [online news article], 13 August 2022, https://www.theguardian.com/environment/2022/aug/23/funding-for-englands-parks-down-330m-a-year-in-real-terms-since-2010, (accessed 7 January 2024).

#01

A standard concrete flag was cut into a C-shape, creating weak points in the paver and leading to apparent cracks.

Every time a standard slab is cut to fit around existing or new elements, such as a bollard or railings, the possibility of creating vulnerable, weak points is high. Therefore, carefully setting out your paving layout beforehand is critical. It is best to minimise cuts by rearranging the paving layout and introducing oversized slabs or to make necessary cuts to reduce weak points.

Laying flags on a flexible sand-based laying course may further exacerbate the problem as pressure from pedestrians and vehicles often creates an uneven base over time that will not support the paving evenly and properly.

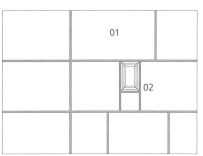

fig. 01

01 – paving slab
02 – bollard

A slab was cut in an L-shape to fit around an existing manhole cover. The difference in settlement between the paving base and the cover added pressure to the weak point in the paver. You can clearly see the resulting tension release cracks.

Carefully setting out the paving is critical, and it is best to minimise cuts by rearranging the paving layout and introducing oversized slabs or make necessary cuts to reduce the tension.

Sometimes using smaller paving units is beneficial if you want to avoid awkward cuts and tricky setting out issues, especially in areas filled with access covers for utilities, bollards and street furniture.

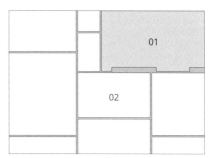

fig. 02

01 – manhole cover
02 – paving slab

#03

Levels and paving go hand in hand. And although a competent contractor can sometimes mask changes in gradients by 'folding' the paving between two different planes, it is important to understand how the varying slopes will affect the paving layout.

In situations where sudden changes in gradients cannot be softened, we recommend using smaller-sized pavers to avoid awkward, unpredicted cuts, a messy layout and ultimately, a weakened paving system.

If the budget allows, one might be able to design and specify bespoke slabs with ridges or slopes on the surface.

Complicated paving patterns that require precise setting out with little tolerance rely on the contractor's talent and the skill of the paviour. It is crucial for a landscape architect to design within budget and the contractor's skills in mind.

The complexity and precision of a line drawing, which often looks convincing on paper, can result in awkward cuts, misalignments and irregular patterns on site.

Simple paving layouts and details that work within a material's physical properties will create long-lasting solutions that age gracefully.

#05

It is common for tactile Yorkstone paving to weather rapidly and, as a result, no longer serve its purpose.

Make yourself familiar with the properties of each stone. Some natural stones are not appropriate for heavy pedestrian traffic. When choosing a material for tactile paving, select a robust and hardy stone that does not erode over time. Most sedimentary rocks like sandstones and limestones are likely to wear fast when exposed to heavy footfall.

Using Yorkstone as a flat paving surface is often not a problem, but any relief or carved-out features will become vulnerable and deteriorate over time. For long-lasting tactile paving, harder stones like granite should be considered.

Alternatively, a replacement strategy must be put in place so that the weathered stones can be easily substituted.

Small stainless steel studs may be installed instead of carved-out blisters, depending on local guidance. Studs may also become loose over time.

Narrow carriageways with inappropriate paving designs can lead to significant failures.

In this example, a heavily trafficked, one-way carriageway coexists next to a designated cycle lane and a pedestrian footpath.

Unfortunately, the colour of the natural stone slabs, blocks and kerbs are very similar to the adjacent road surface, making it difficult for drivers to see the roadway. In addition, the shallow kerbs and insufficient build-ups made the surfaces vulnerable to heavy vehicles, resulting in a failed paving system and patchwork repairs.

Engineers should always check road and paving build-ups, while designers should consider vehicular build-ups in pavements for shared surfaces. The indicative section (fig. 03) shows the appropriate below-ground construction layers for this condition.

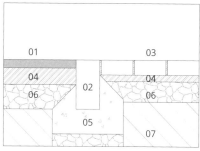

fig. 03

01 – natural stone paving slabs
02 – natural stone kerb
03 – natural stone paving blocks
04 – bedding layer
05 – concrete base*
06 – compacted granular sub-base layer*
07 – compacted subgrade layer*
*thickness to be determined based on the anticipated loading and existing ground conditions

In this example, the designers ignored the alignment of joints between the steps and the wall. Aligning steps and cladding can be tricky, especially if the two elements do not meet at a 90-degree angle. Fig. 04 demonstrates how simple adjustments to the cladding can improve the situation without increasing construction costs.

The second issue with this detail is the inconsistent joints that appear when the cladding overhangs the steps and paving. This type of detail pressures the contractor to cut the cladding perfectly to achieve a consistent parallel joint.

It is best practice to run a vertical element behind the steps and below the surface to create a horizontal joint rather than a vertical one.

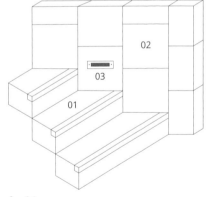

fig. 04

01 – step
02 – cladding stone
03 – light fitting

A movement joint was installed between two walls, but an isolation joint between the hard landscape and the wall is missing.

The project team failed to consider differential movement between the two elements, resulting in a large crack that widened over time. The problem can be easily fixed by replacing the grout with a mastic filler.

It is easier and cheaper to prevent this issue during the design phase. Not all building interfaces require a movement joint, but it is worth asking the engineers for their advice.

It's worth noting that colours available on the market for mastic is relatively limited compared to mortar, so it is wise to test how this detail looks in a mock-up.

#09

We see these kinds of mistakes often in new schemes. Although joint layouts and threshold design aren't the sexiest things to care about, they can be pretty jarring if not designed and built correctly.

The coordination of construction information between various disciplines is critical, as are discussions with contractors to explain the design intent and site visits to keep track of progress. Often, many site issues can be addressed if a degree of flexibility is built into the design.

In this instance, a number of oversized slabs, discussions with the contractor about setting out or a simplified paving design could have prevented this misalignment.

Sometimes the root of a problem exposes itself by simply looking at it. In this example, granite setts laid in a stack bond (grid), have slowly turned in the direction of the traffic.

Building a rigid paving system isn't always enough for heavily trafficked areas. In this example, we recommend using an interlocking pattern for a stronger paving system.

#11

#12

Just a reminder to clear the drains occasionally, especially as some of them prevent water from entering the building.

Although obvious but all too often not implemented, always check that all drainage outlets are connected to existing pipes, attenuation tanks, etc.

Levels and drainage around entrances, especially secondary ones, are often forgotten and left uncoordinated until the last minute. For new builds, it is crucial to understand the various regulations that dictate access requirements in and out of a building and how to deal with potential water ingress.

Although this appears to be a service entrance, not part of a fire escape route and therefore less critical, the difference in level between the internal floor and the pavement creates an awkward recessed area that will inevitably pool. Not to mention the impossibility of fully opening the door.

Surface water drainage and paving levels should be coordinated at every project stage between the landscape architect, the engineers and the architect.

3D modelling tools for complex locations can help you visualise the terrain. The detailed topographical survey of the site should assist you with merging your proposals with the existing streetscape. In addition, surface water drainage needs to consider ownership boundaries, guidelines and regulations related to water discharge and attenuation.

In this instance, the choice of drainage outlet is critical. A linear slot drain at the bottom of the steps would have easily prevented water from pooling, no matter the surrounding falls.

#14

When paving meets a curved edge, particular care and attention is needed to avoid large triangular gaps filled with mortar or the need for thinly cut infill pieces that are likely to break.

The size, pattern and setting out of paving should be carefully considered for paving blocks only to be cut slightly and eliminating gaps or small cut blocks (fig. 05). However, there is still a risk of compromising the blocks' structural integrity by changing the L x W x H ratio. This may result in future cracks, especially in heavily trafficked areas.

It is good practice to consider oversized blocks to create neatly cut edges on site (fig. 06). Allow for enough excess material so the cut line can be adjusted according to setting out on site.

01 – paving blocks
02 – curved steel edge
03 – stone blocks cut to follow the curve

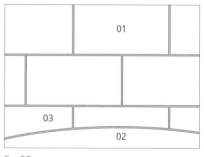

fig. 05

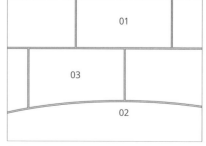

fig. 06

When developing the paving and drainage design, always consider how they will be set out to avoid awkward relationships.

To avoid these issues, develop the levels and drainage strategy with the paving and edges in mind. Often, below-ground constraints and necessary surface falls can limit how drains and gulleys can be set out.

If possible, it is best for a slot drain or any other drainage type to align with the general direction of the paving and with the edges of the slabs. This solution (fig. 07) minimises the number of cuts and maintains an appropriate L x W x H ratio for pavers while improving the alignment of the slot drain.

When smaller block paving units or setts are used on a project, it is worth considering gullies instead of linear drains to minimise on-site cuts, reduce visual impact and make setting out easier.

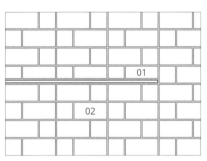

fig. 07

01 – slot drain
02 – paving blocks

#16

Every slot drain needs an outlet point at the end of a run for rodding and maintenance. These small covers are often overlooked during the design process and should be set out to avoid vulnerable awkward or irregular cuts in the paving.

Equally, a mitre joint on a narrow kerb corner can be a weak detail, especially if exposed to unexpected pedestrian or vehicular traffic.

Fig. 08 shows how simple adjustments to the kerb's corner and the setting out of the access cover can prevent these mistakes.

It is also wise to consider how the paving system moves and applies pressure to edges, drains and covers. Specifying mastic joints between these elements is good practice to allow for differential movement.

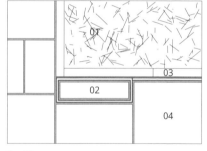

fig. 08

01 – vegetation
02 – access cover with infill stone
03 – kerb
04 – paving slab

Slot drains are an elegant alternative to traditional drains, but they can be more susceptible to the movement of the surrounding paving system.

In rigid, hard landscape construction, it is vital to consider the expansion and contraction of the paving system and how it affects interfaces.

Always coordinate with a civil engineer to produce a robust, hard-wearing paving design. Engineers will help you set out the various types of joints according to your paving pattern and interfaces.

In this scenario, and for slot drains in general, we recommend placing it away from a movement line or using mastic joints on both sides of the slot drain's throat to allow the paving system to 'breath' without compressing the drain.

#18

If installed correctly, recessed covers are discrete and invisible to passers-by. They are a great solution to providing 'invisible' access to services and utilities running beneath the paving.

In this example, we suspect that a newly paved area was laid over existing manholes which were ignored during the design and/or construction process. For covers to be laid in the correct direction, the manhole below should either be rotated or fitted to allow a new cover to be placed in a different position/orientation.

We would also recommend installing a cover with discrete lifting points. Depending on the paver sizes and pattern, these can come in various shapes and sizes. In this example, small square lifting points in the corners would have better suited the design.

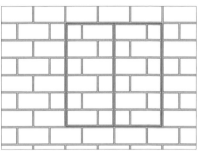

fig. 09

As per the previous example, recessed covers can be discrete if they are installed in line with the paving pattern and paver sizes. Sometimes, a project's budget will not allow existing manholes to be changed or rotated in line with the new design.

In this case, the paving inside the cover could have been installed in the same direction as the surrounding paving, minimising the cover's visibility.

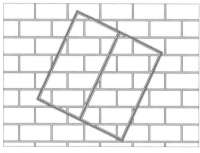

fig. 10

#20

In public spaces, stainless steel grills can be great as a walkable surface over drainage, tree pits and vents. Sadly, they are also great for hiding rubbish.

In this example, a grill was installed next to a seating edge, making it very tempting for people to squeeze a pack of crisps or cigarettes between the grills.

A tree pit in paving is a system of many parts that must be carefully considered and coordinated, especially if the soil extends underneath the surface, beyond the visible pit.

A tree pit should allow a tree, its rooting system and soil to breathe to ensure the plant's long-term health. It is, therefore, crucial to install vents to aerate the soil below, let gases escape and allow oxygen to reach the tree's rooting area. These vents also provide another access point for watering the tree and soil below.

This case study is a reminder to consider how the tree pit system integrates with the layout of the paving. This reminder also extends to recessed tree uplights that often form part of the pit.

Equally important is the consideration of the tree grill and the 'collar' design around the trunk. In standard tree grill designs, a gap is left between the trunk and the grill, allowing the tree to grow.

However, this leaves a relatively wide gap which can become a trip hazard in busy pedestrian areas. Often, this gap is filled with aggregates, but one must remember to consider their size, so that they don't travel easily and get stuck in the grills.

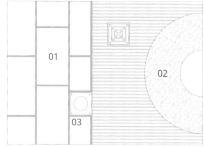

fig. 11

01 – paving slab
02 – gravel
03 – uplight

#22

The paving inside this recessed manhole cover has caved in under the pressure of heavy vehicles running over it.

Recessed stainless steel manhole covers are great when trying to hide access points in newly paved areas. However, several factors have to be considered. First, the cover should be designed to withstand the expected vehicular loads. The recess has to be deep enough to allow for a bedding layer and the paver depth. A chemically fixed thinner slab can sometimes be used under occasional light loading.

Wherever feasible, avoid placing manholes in heavily trafficked areas or, alternatively, use a more robust cast iron cover.

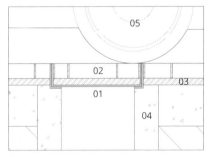

fig. 12

01 – recessed cover
02 – paving blocks
03 – bedding layer
04 – concrete foundations
05 – car

Our streets and public spaces are built over layers of buried utilities and services accumulated over centuries.

Landscape architects should seek to incorporate survey information into their designs and work around services that are unlikely to be relocated. Timely coordination with MEP and civil engineers will result in a more integrated and coherent layout.

Often, large-scale urban projects have the capacity to rationalise existing below-ground services, eliminate redundant runs or replace aged ducts and cables. The budget and implications on the construction sequence should be carefully assessed at the beginning of the project.

However, it is sometimes impossible to know what sits below the site, and a few surprises may appear during demolition. This example is a reminder to always stay flexible and keep an open mind when encountering clashes later in the design process.

#24

Perennial species planted in recessed manhole covers are unlikely to establish or survive, especially if the manhole below needs to be accessed on a regular basis.

Recessed manhole covers are designed for paving and are usually too shallow for planting (and often do not have a drainage outlet). Newly planted perennials might survive in these conditions for the first year but won't be able to develop a good root system over time. The soil within the recessed cover will also dry out much faster or stay waterlogged.

Most landscape and public realm projects in urban environments will have below-ground services running beneath them. It is difficult to avoid them altogether, but it is certainly possible to design with or around them.

If the cover cannot be moved to a paved area, it is best to use simple cast iron covers that blend with the surrounding soil and mulch layer. Even better, it should be set deeper within the planting bed so it can be hidden. You may want to consider planting taller, spreading evergreen species to hide the cover all year round.

Sometimes a picture is worth a thousand words. The seat is too low and too small (although maybe originally intended for children), and it is located on a corner where people are unlikely to sit.

The steel retaining edge looks sharp, sticks out and does not follow the profile of the soil. This detail is potentially dangerous.

As for the paving, the brick tooth edge detail looks vulnerable and will break over time.

We see no solution nor easy fixes other than rebuilding this area.

#26

This is quite a common mistake that we see in public parks and gardens. It is best to avoid placing seating against lawn as foot traffic will inevitably destroy the grass and compact the soil over time. We recommend installing an area paving against the bench.

This curved bench features laser-cut Cor-ten side panels filled with reused construction rubble. Although it may be an interesting concept, in practice, the design has proven vulnerable to anti-social behaviour. The gaps between pieces of rubble are constantly filled with litter. And the overall geometry of the bench means that it leaves small, hard-to-maintain areas that also often fill up with rubbish.

#28

One can be creative with public benches. Thinking of who, how and when people socialise or relax outside can inspire a multitude of playful, elegant and/or functional designs.

Successful benches and their arrangement, can significantly improve one's experience of a public square, park or street. They help bring people together, provide a comfortable vantage point to watch the world go by and support those of us that need a rest.

Unfortunately, awkward designs can have the opposite effect.

It is completely puzzling why anyone would want to sit on this narrow, littered stretch of grass, stuck in the middle of a very busy dual carriageway. Could this be a solution to avoid anti-social gatherings?

Good-quality seating is crucial in our cities. Sadly, they are often poorly designed, misplaced and/or arranged in awkward positions.

#30

Watching passers-by while sitting under a tree on a warm summer's day can be considered one of life's great pleasures. But it is important to remember that we share our public spaces with other creatures who also have a favourite pastime of their own.

We've noticed that bird faeces dissolve powder coating over time. So it might be wise to omit 'sensitive' finishes during the design stage or ensure that the maintenance regime is adequate when placing street furniture under a tree.

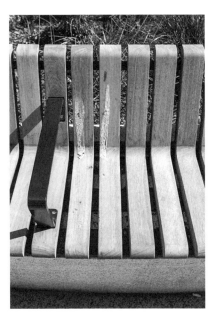

A bench placed below a mature tree will need to be cleaned regularly due to bird droppings.

Pigeons, so common in our cities, can also frequent the same quiet urban parks and courtyards we enjoy.

Droppings can make any seating surface dirty and will require a daily cleaning regime. Carefully considering existing trees and placing benches away from large overhanging branches can help the issue.

Anti-skating measures were installed for this bespoke stone bench, however the detail wasn't robust enough and failed.

In an urban setting, designers often use the most durable materials and add anti-skating measures when designing street furniture. For example, a series of carved granite recesses along the bench edge could be a good option, but it should be tested in a mock-up to confirm size, depth and regularity.

In some instances, it is worth considering a rough/ textured paved surface around the bench to deter skateboarders from jumping and grinding on it. A cropped stone finish or loose gravel will make the areas less desirable to skateboarders.

#33

When placing benches against planting beds, ensure enough seating space is available to prevent plants from getting damaged. In this example, the 450-500mm wide bench isn't wide enough for people to sit comfortably without touching and damaging the plants, leaving large bare areas of soil.

Widening the bench would have allowed more space for people to sit, while allowing plants to grow over the planter's edge. Installing a backrest would also help protect the plants behind.

The rubber edge cover on top of the planter could have been avoided by simply folding the steel (see #99).

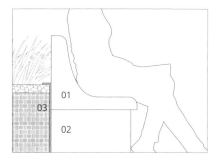

fig. 13

01 – seat with a backrest
02 – bench base
03 – planter

This elaborate 'bug hotel' is a great example of a shallow pledge to support biodiversity. The hotel completely fails to appreciate the requirements and science behind man-made wildlife habitats.

A 'bug hotel' needs to be located away from prevailing winds, provide a degree of cover from the rain and have a back cover. Placed away from the ground below the trees might be beneficial for solitary bees, but the insufficient depth of the nesting holes and the exposed location will prevent them from choosing this place, while other insects will struggle to find this shelter suspended above a green roof and ventilation grill. Not many insects naturally coexist together and some of the selected organic debris can also attract unwanted predators.

The suspended cable system needs to be checked on an annual basis to prevent damage to the trees and may cause repeated damage during windy days. On balance, this example of a man-made habitat will bring no benefit and may even cause harm.

#35

A wealth of information on street furniture design is readily available online. Local authorities, government and non-government bodies all share guidance and technical advice on their websites. From bus shelters and parking designs to street trees and cycle stands, the public realm is exhaustively regulated to provide designers and contractors with the right tools to create a functional outdoor environment.

For this case study, imagining how people park their bicycles and some common sense would have prevented racks being installed too close to a wall.

External finishes in public spaces are vulnerable to wear and tear. Most metal coatings will scratch and/or wear off over time depending on usage, anti-social behaviour and weather. Cycle stands in particular tend to lose their finish quickly.

The most forgiving and robust materials for cycle stands are galvanised steel, stainless steel or Cor-ten. Depending on your budget and design considerations, any of these metals will be your best bet to avoid maintenance issues.

#37

Stainless steel furniture and lighting fixtures can often be damaged by rust when installed with inappropriate fixings.

It is crucial to understand how materials react to each other and how various metals perform under exposed conditions. In this example, long-term damage could have been avoided if the baseplate had been fixed with a complimentary metal, such as stainless steel.

This lamp post's concrete pad was cast too close to the surface and is now left exposed, creating a trip hazard.

The finished levels of all buried foundations should be coordinated with surface levels, allowing enough build-up to cover the foundations. In unique and shallow conditions, it is sometimes best to simply draw a section to understand depths and tolerances.

On a sloping site, like the example above, it is necessary to place foundations deeper than the norm, as the chosen surface above will likely settle and move over time.

#39

This steel post was placed after the paving was installed. Core-drilled and filled with concrete, the foundation not only appears at the surface but seem to fail. Not sturdy enough against people and vehicles bashing into it, the concrete foundation is moving, leading to cracks in the stone. For retrofitting a post, it is best to lift the paver, pour adequate foundation and re-set the paving around it, thus covering the concrete.

An ornamental shrub is planted in a pot under the soffit of a new building. Its form and scale are inappropriate for the location: the top branches are touching the soffit, the plant shows signs of decay, and the amount of light and water is limited.

This is one example where no planting would have been better than any planting. When considering plant and tree species, pay attention to scale, form, final size, environmental conditions and how the scheme will be maintained.

#41

#42

A protection grill is damaging this young, struggling tree. Since this is a feathered tree with branches growing at low height, the barrier is restricting its growth, causing irreparable harm.

Typically, young feathered pines should not be planted as street trees. This slow-growing, low canopy specimen is likely to get vandalised or accidentally damaged by pedestrians and vehicles. Although a barrier/cage is a good idea to protect standard trees in busy locations, in this instance, it is extremely restrictive and detrimental to the tree's ability to establish in an urban environment.

Street trees perform best when they are planted already semi-mature/mature with a minimum clear stem of 2m. A protective fence can be used as a temporary measure to safeguard the trunk before it reaches the appropriate girth. No branches should be restricted by the barrier.

This tree is showing signs of stress and premature decay as it is planted in a small pit with limited soil volume and too close to the façade.

As its proximity to the building prevents access to and maintenance of the façade, it must be heavily pruned, further deteriorating the tree's health and appearance.

Even small columnar trees such as this one should be planted at least 3m away from a building's façade.

Soil volume for street trees is equally important, and with the help of structural cells or tree sand, the soil should be extended below the paving.

At the surface, the exposed tree pit area should be protected with a recessed cover, resin-bound gravel or loose gravel to avoid heavy compaction.

A classic example of 'not my job'. The tree pit was cut diagonally to the paving pattern. It is very unlikely that this was a deliberate design proposal and most certainly a lack of coordination between the people on site and the design team. The absence of a tree grill and the awkward relationship with the manhole covers makes the image even more disturbing.

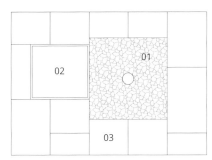

fig. 14

01 – resin-bound gravel
02 – recessed manhole cover
03 – paving slabs

#44

Tree roots can be quite difficult to constrain, especially if the size of the pit doesn't account for the future root zone. Although root barriers should be installed around the pit, this very common scenario will inevitably occur if the area was designed too small.

Ask arboriculturists, tree nurseries or tree pit systems suppliers for advice on species and appropriate pit sizes as some trees naturally tend to have shallow roots.

Sadly, we see this quite often in cities. Newly planted trees are, time and time again, inadequate for the environment they sit in. Regarding age and shape, we generally recommend semi-mature to mature single-stem trees in busy streets, with a minimum of 2m clearance between the ground and foliage. While this clearance ensures that the smaller, more vulnerable branches and foliage are harder to reach, the single thick stem is harder to bend or break.

In this example, thousands of people will brush against this small strawberry tree. It is also multi-stemmed and therefore easier to snap, even inadvertently. The choice of species is therefore crucial. The right tree depends on climatic conditions, pit size, surrounding surfaces, proximity to traffic and buildings, water run-off and maintenance regime (among others). Many organisations offer advice and online guidance, such as the Trees and Design Action Group database (UK).

For this tree, we believe the problem to be the opposite. Several 15–17m tall mature deciduous trees were planted incorrectly. Having witnessed the project's construction, we noticed the trees had not been air-potted. In most cases, such mature trees must be lifted out of the ground and air-potted a few years prior. This reduces stress and slowly helps them transition from field conditions to an urban tree pit.

The more mature the tree, the more sensitive it can be to sudden environmental changes. It is, therefore, essential to properly prepare a tree in advance and take extra care during and after its planting.

The following summer was remarkably hot and dry. The lack of extra monitoring and watering exacerbated the problem, with cracks appearing along the main stems. This particular location being also very windy, any large tree would have struggled to survive.

#47

These neglected tree pits are unsuitable for new trees.

The size of a proposed tree pit should relate to the size of the specified tree. In this instance, this 800 x 800mm tree pit can only fit a small 400mm diametre root ball or a bare-root specimen that will not grow very tall.

In urban conditions, where trees are planted in paved areas and access to air, water and nutrients is limited, good soil volume and maintenance are critical.

Compacted soil, pollution and limited root space can dramatically reduce a tree's chances of survival.

Although some species are more resilient and suitable to urban conditions than others (*Platanus x hispanica, Gleditsia tiracanthos, Ginko biloba*, for example), all tree pits should be carefully planned and designed. Structural soil cells or specialist urban tree soils should be specified to aid tree growth.

A tree must be planted soon after a tree pit is prepared to avoid soil compaction, contamination and waste. For pavements, it is wise to consider a tree pit cover that prevents soil compaction and damage to the root ball over time.

Significant dents and dips appear around these tree pits. This is because the soil, which extends underneath the surrounding surface, appears to have settled more than anticipated, creating apparent undulations above.

However, this issue is not just a settlement problem between the various build-ups underneath (between the soil for the tree and the artificial turf's permeable build-up). It reveals that the project team did not anticipate how the tree could be replaced if it ever died.

When designing a tree pit, planning for a worst-case scenario is essential. In this example, the root ball is allowed to extend below the surface, but it is apparent that significant and costly remedial works will be required in case the tree fails.

Not only do we recommend using a specialist structural soil designed for tree pits under walkable surfaces, but the size of the opening should also reflect the roots' future spread.

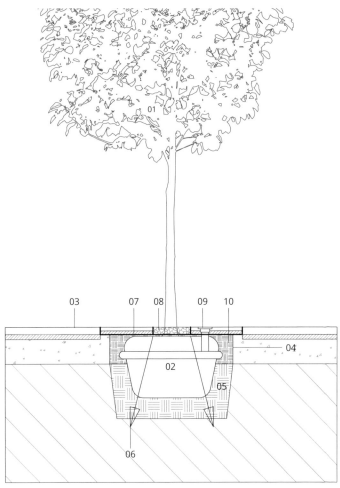

fig. 15

01 – tree
02 – root ball
03 – paving slabs
04 – hard landscape edge to be neatly cut or shuttered to maximise space for roots
05 – subsoil

06 – below-ground anchoring system
07 – recessed steel tray with paving slabs cut to fit
08 – loose gravel around the trunk
09 – irrigation pipe
10 – topsoil

The tree pit is set out perpendicular to the kerb line while the paving pattern runs perpendicular to the building's façade, resulting in an unfortunate and overcomplicated joint layout.

Fig. 16 offers an alternative layout that makes it easier to lay the paving, creates fewer cuts and appears intentional. Understanding how things are built on site and knowing the construction sequence can help you spot issues before they cause a problem.

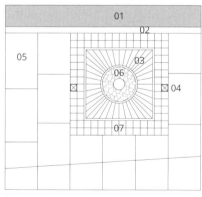

fig. 16

01 – road surface
02 – stone kerb
03 – steel grill cover
04 – irrigation/aeration pipe
05 – paving slab
06 – gravel
07 – stone setts

#50

A chestnut tree has outgrown its original planter. The future health of a tree is jeopardised if its root system is limited by a constrained pit. Similarly, a planter can collapse and break under the force of a tree's roots. Always make sure to plan for the right pit size according to the species.

This is an excellent example of how a tree's final growth, girth and root system wasn't considered in the design of the tree pit. Poor tree pit design can create messy streetscapes, cracked paving and poor tree health over time.

Frequently, designers forget that even urban trees can have a prolonged life expectancy and grow far larger than expected. Some species are also known to develop strong roots that grow close to the surface and will lift the pavement above.

In constrained areas with heavy pedestrian traffic, paved tree grill covers can be designed with detachable panels that can be easily removed as the tree grows.

#52

#53

A tree was planted in a small, raised brick planter, which ultimately collapsed.

Trees can break any hard landscape materials over time. Therefore, a tree's ultimate growth should always be considered when planting a tree in a raised planter. The solidity of the raised edges is also critical in avoiding future issues.

In this example, a steel edge with welded or prefabricated corner pieces or a cast solid reinforced concrete edge would work better. However, the planter size would need to be increased and possibly a series of root directors installed to control the spread of the root system.

A tree was planted too close to an existing brick wall. Over time, it undermined the wall's structural integrity, resulting in a partial collapse.

Sufficient distance between new trees and vertical structures, buildings or foundations is critical, as it ensures the structure's integrity and the tree's ability to develop a strong root system. In addition, we recommend installing root barriers against any below-ground structures or utilities to limit a tree's roots.

The tree pit was covered with recycled broken concrete slabs bound by a cement mix that prevents air and water from accessing the root system.

This unnecessary design was likely an ad hoc attempt by the maintenance team to create a more robust tree pit cover to minimise the need for maintenance in the future. Unfortunately, this solution prevents surface water and air from penetrating to the tree's roots, thus constraining the trunk's growth.

Using rubberised mulch or self-binding gravel offers a more long-term solution in this condition.

#55

This cast-iron tree grill cover has an insufficiently sized opening that did not consider the tree's future growth and expansion.

Grills are an excellent tool for widening pavements in dense urban settings. It is important to remember that their weight should be distributed away from the root ball. And as the tree becomes established, this cover should be removed or substituted with a larger one.

This tree was planted too close to a road kerb, creating long-term maintenance issues.

The London plane (*Platanus x hispanica*) is one of Europe's most popular urban trees. They are tough, have a long lifespan, and can be easily pollarded and shaped to work in many different urban conditions.

A London plane can grow up to 30m high, and its trunk can achieve a girth of over 2m. Therefore, it is crucial to carefully place young trees away from buildings, structures and, as in this case, road kerbs.

Alternative tree species should be considered when the street profile doesn't allow enough space for a large tree canopy. Refer to a helpful guide from TDAG for further information.

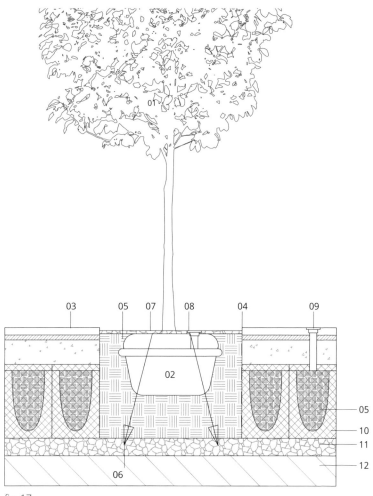

fig. 17

01 – tree
02 – root ball dimension will vary
depending on the tree size
03 – paving slabs
04 – hard landscape edge to be neatly cut
or shuttered to maximise space for roots
05 – structural soil

06 – below-ground anchoring system
07 – gravel mulch
08 – irrigation pipe
09 – aeration pipe
10 – structural soil cells
11 – gravel layer
12 – subgrade

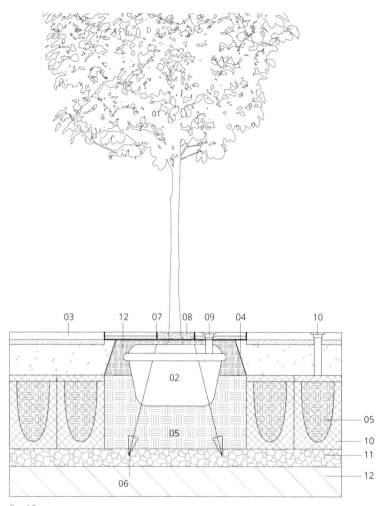

fig. 18

01 – tree
02 – root ball dimension will vary
depending on the tree size
03 – paving slabs
04 – root barrier
05 – subsoil
06 – below-ground anchoring system

07 – recessed steel tray with paving slabs
cut to fit
08 – loose gravel around the trunk
09 – irrigation pipe
10 – aeration pipe
11 – structural soil cells
12 – topsoil
13 – subgrade

#57

Certain tree species, like ornamental cherries, tend to develop shallow root systems that can lift the paving and bound surfaces.

These species should be avoided in hard landscaped areas, or a larger tree pit should be designed with a flexible surface cover. In addition, a degree of ongoing yearly maintenance should be considered.

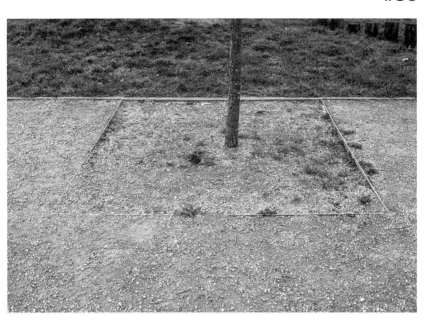

This steel edge around the tree pit is unnecessary. It can even become a trip hazard and a maintenance issue in the future.

It is possible to achieve a seamless transition between tree pits and footpaths with self-binding surfaces. This will create a pleasant, informal atmosphere similar to classic French gardens.

However, allowing people to walk close to the trees can lead to soil compaction around the root balls. We recommend planting a tree in structural urban soil with a layer of self-binding gravel on top. The same soil can be used as a sub-base below the surrounding gravel areas. Alternatively, a grid of structural tree cells can be installed to provide a nutrient-rich layer of topsoil while avoiding compaction over time.

#59

This example shows a sinking tree pit surrounded by a cracked resin-bound surface with a shallow aluminium edge set in excessive concrete.

The project team did not consider how the tree would be removed and replaced easily if it died. It is crucial to ensure that the extent of the tree pit at surface level matches the soil below. In this example, the square formed by the aluminium edge should have been much larger. Inside, aggregates or a permeable resin surface could be installed over the root ball with structural soil or cells below to avoid compaction over time.

If the intention is to leave the tree pit open, we recommend installing a deeper aluminium or steel edge so that the concrete it sits on does not appear above the soil.

Above-ground tree stakes are often forgotten and neglected post-installation. Displaced stakes serve no function and will damage the bark of the tree. Fig. 19 shows a typical tree stake detail that can be used temporarily until the tree's roots are fully developed.

In this case, the above-ground stakes were installed poorly, providing insufficient support and damaging the tree. Fig. 19 shows a typical tree stake detail that can be used temporarily until the tree's roots are fully developed.

#62

#63

A stainless steel CCTV warning sign was attached to a tree with a metal tension tie. The tie was left for an extended period without being adjusted as the tree grew, severely damaging the trunk and potentially killing the tree.

It is important to remember that nothing should be permanently fixed to trees, especially young ones. In addition, no metal bracings, ties or other sharp-edged fixings that can damage the bark should ever be used. Appropriate protective rubber or fabric is recommended if you need to fix a temporary sign or luminaire.

A stake was placed very close to a tree's trunk, the rubber tie was fastened too tightly, and the whole system was left in place for too long.

After providing some initial support, the tie now strangles the trunk, causing irreversible damage. In addition, stakes and tie were installed incorrectly, and the maintenance team neglected to maintain the system as the tree outgrew the initial installation.

Pending a tree's successful establishment and growth, all tree stakes must generally be removed after 2–3 years.

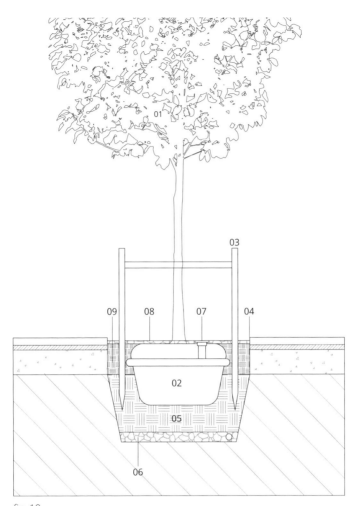

fig. 19

01 – tree
02 – root ball
03 – temporary above-ground stakes, to be removed after a couple of years, ties to be checked regularly, especially after heavy winds
04 – hard landscape edge to be neatly cut or shuttered to maximise space for roots
05 – subsoil
06 – additional gravel layer at the bottom of a tree pit might be required depending on the permeability of the sub-base
07 – irrigation pipe
08 – bark or gravel mulch layer laid slightly below the finished paving level is the best material to allow air and water circulation; to avoid soil compaction in urban sites, resin-bound gravel or recessed tree grills could be considered
09 – topsoil

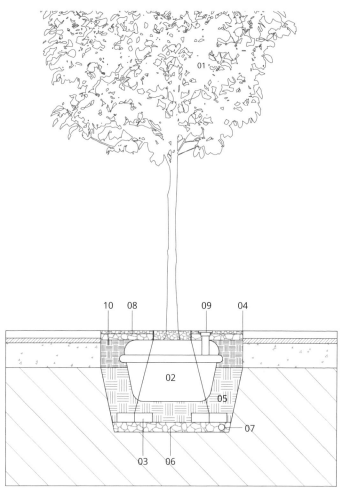

fig. 20

01 – tree
02 – root ball
03 – below-ground dead man anchoring system
04 – hard landscape edge to be neatly cut or shuttered to maximise space for roots
05 – subsoil
06 – additional gravel layer at the bottom of a tree pit might be required depending on the permeability of the sub-base
07 – perforated drainage pipe can improve drainage in heavily congested urban sites
08 – resin-bound gravel layer and compacted aggregates
09 – irrigation pipe
10 – topsoil

Not all tree species are suitable for the streets—particularly near tall vehicles such as vans and double-decker buses. Always check local authority guidance for recommended species and specifications to avoid misshapen and deformed trees in the future. Specifying a tree with the correct stem clearance would have been more adequate for this location.

#65

Exposing a root ball is never a good idea. Even with an automatic irrigation system, the tree will struggle to survive long term.

Knowing root ball sizes is critical at the very early stages of a project. Understanding the required soil depth for different trees will ensure their healthy establishment and future growth.

Constrained urban conditions limit the equal spread of a tree's root ball over time. Besides allowing for below-ground anchors or above-ground stakes, one must consider services and foundations below. Drawing a detailed section with the correct root ball dimensions confirmed by the nursery can flesh out clashes before the project is on site. Sometimes a small tree is more likely to fit into a constrained area and will probably grow and establish faster.

This is a typical example of a tree breaking the paving due to poor detailing and installation. It appears that concrete pavers were laid directly above the soil of the tree pit, which looks too small for the tree. Not only was the paving laid on the wrong base, but it was also installed too close to the trunk and above the roots.

We recommend removing the damaged pavers and any other slab above the tree pit as a temporary measure. One could then install a porous surface that is suitable for pedestrian use and allows water and air to reach the roots.

Installing permeable paving or resin-bound gravel could be a good permanent solution for this case study. For a new tree pit, however, we recommend using a tree grill that spans the pit length to avoid compaction of the soil over time due to pedestrian traffic.

#67

#68

Planting on a steep slope failed due to a lack of irrigation and maintenance. Trying to establish any vegetation on slopes with a gradient over 1:3 is challenging. Not only do we recommend soil stabilisation solutions (as implemented in this example), but additional irrigation is necessary for the plants to cope with the quickly draining substrate.

In this example, an almost vertical wall of clipped *Lonicera nitida* was planted. Typically, these plants will require moist but well-drained soil to thrive. A series of connected gabion-like baskets with soil wrapped in a filter fleece was used to provide the necessary growing environment for the plants. Over time, nutrients washed away and the automatic irrigation system temporarily failed, quickly resulting in plants dying.

A different choice of species that naturally grows on poor, dry, steep and rocky slopes would have been a better fit for this location.

Different climbing plants utilise a variety of methods to support themselves when climbing up structures.

There are species with leaf or stem tendrils or twining growing habits to attach themselves to various supports and structures. Others use adhesive pads or clinging stem roots. It is important to learn and understand these various growing habits when specifying a green wall to provide the appropriate support system or façade.

In this example, a stainless steel grid mesh does not help the Hydrangeas, as they use stem roots to attach themselves to a vertical surface.

Freshly installed pre-grown turf mats failed due to a lack of watering. Automatic irrigation systems are extremely useful in urban conditions where heat, limited soil volumes and natural cover create hostile conditions for plants to thrive.

An irrigation system can dramatically reduce the need for manual maintenance and keep your plants looking great all year round. Initial installation costs can be easily justified when long-term site maintenance is considered. The irrigation is calibrated to only use the amount of water necessary for the plants and can prevent manual over-watering and/or irregular supply.

Pre-grown turf is great for an instant lawn. It should be regularly irrigated in the beginning to allow for the fibrous routes to develop. Access onto the lawn should be limited before it is fully established.

In areas where water supply is limited or biodiversity is important, alternatives to traditional lawns should be explored. Species-rich seed mixes, tapestry lawns, mixed ground covers or wildflower meadows are great alternatives.

#70

#71

A green wall is a fantastic tool to cover a blank façade. Most of them are made of small, irrigated planters stacked above each other. The irrigation system allows for a wide range of species to thrive in places otherwise inhabitable to plants.

The limited soil volume in each planter means that the plants are reliant on the nutrients in the irrigation water. As such, green walls heavily rely on automated irrigation systems to survive.

It is important to understand that green walls will fail as soon as the irrigation malfunctions or nutrients aren't replenished. Therefore, the entire system is reliant on a strict maintenance regime over time.

Although hard to see on this image, the wall features a mixture of real and fake plants. We assume the fake plants were installed as the real climber did not cover the wall completely. Always remember to specify the right species according to sun exposure, soil volume, wall type and maintenance regime.

In this example, the soil sits too low against the building and the paving edge. Since the planting beds are on a steep slope, we suspect the soil slowly eroded over time.

As a temporary measure, more soil could be added and groundcovers planted to help raise the soil's shear strength.

Where proposed ground levels are unavoidably steep, soil retention mesh or a higher retaining edge should be installed at the bottom of the slope.

When installing soil against a building's façade, discuss interface details with the design team to find an appropriate solution. For example, specifying a waterproofing/drainage layer/membrane will prevent moisture build-up and damage to the cladding.

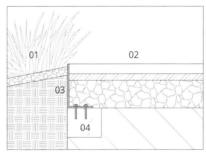

fig. 21

01 – planting
02 – paving slab
03 – steel or aluminium edge
04 – concrete foundation

#73

#74

This evergreen hedge was severely pruned at the bottom and left unclipped at the top, beyond the cutter's reach. The damaged lower section is unlikely to regrow, while the section above will remain irregular.

In constrained urban conditions, it is important to consider a plant's habit, its growing preferences, ultimate height and spread to prevent an unsightly result and costly or complicated maintenance operations.

This example shows how a Leyland cypress (*Cupressus leylandii*) isn't fit for this location and maintenance regime. The fast-growing plant can reach up to 12m in height and an 8m spread in just 10 years. An alternative species like English yew (*Taxus baccata*) could have been a better choice as it is more slow-growing and responds well to hard pruning when left uncut.

This overgrown hedge is spilling out onto the pavement, seriously narrowing circulation space.

Very often, people forget to consider a plant's mature size. Many species can grow dramatically large if planted in the right conditions and maintained correctly. Knowing a species' habits and size at maturity beforehand will prevent any unnecessary maintenance in the future.

In this instance, the hedge was planted too close to the footpath and was allowed to grow out over the pavement. Some plants respond well to hard pruning and can be brought back to the desired size.

This poor tree features a damaged and crooked branch. All trees should be supervised by a professional during installation and, if damaged, they should be pruned and treated.

Due to its contorted branch, this tree should not have been selected at the nursery or rejected when delivered to site.

This newly planted tree is growing at an angle due to extreme local wind conditions. Dense urban developments often create specific micro-climates. Desktop-based simulations and wind tunnel tests will help with the specie selection. Certain species can cope with windy conditions, but to increase their chances of survival, these need to be germinated and grown under the same conditions.

Time scales on most projects do not allow such lengthy procurement routes, and clients often ask for fully grown plants for instant impact. Unfortunately, this means containerised trees will not have a strong, spreading root system to help anchor themselves. As a result, it is crucial to specify below-ground anchors or above-ground stakes. Even with an achoring system, establishing new trees in very windy conditions is likely to fail. Closely planted groups of small resilient trees are more likely to succeed in sites with moderate winds.

#77

Greening a plant room is an excellent idea until maintenance fails to keep the green wall alive. Any green wall requires constant monitoring, daily irrigation and frequent replacement of plants and soil.

In this example, the large planting bed set against the plant room looks ideal for growing climbing plants. Several self-clinging plants or twining specimens growing on a support frame or trellis would create a green wall that requires little maintenance.

Climbing plants are the most sustainable vertical greening system and should always be considered first.

Is the designer responsible for specifying such a large hedge too close to the bench? Or did the maintenance team fail to prune the plants?

It is important to remember that the maintenance of a public space inevitably varies over time. In public spaces, there is little guarantee that the specified maintenance regime will be implemented post-completion. The original vision for the planting is often not passed down to the various maintenance teams who take care of the space over time. Nor do the responsible authorities have time to supervise and uphold the original design intent.

In many cases, it is best to plan for the worst and consider, and design for, the mature size of plants and how they appear if unkept. In this situation, we recommend specifying a plant with a more upright growth habit or placing the hedge further away from the bench.

#79

Pedestrian desire lines can lead to unsightly paths, loss of vegetation and ongoing maintenance problems.

When designing public spaces, it is necessary to consider existing and future desire lines and allow necessary space for various means of movement. In this instance, a strong informal footpath was created through areas of grass when a new residential development was built on the edge of an existing public park.

The impact of the residential development on the surrounding context should have been discussed during planning application meetings, leading to simple adjustments to the park layout.

As per the previous case study, desire lines can create unsightly paths through planting beds. It is unfortunate that these two access covers are placed perfectly in the middle of a desire line.

For this case study, we aren't sure if the topsoil disappeared, was compacted over time or was never there in the first place. Judging by the look of the soil in this picture, it appears to be sandy subsoil with large aggregates, a growing medium unsuitable for most plants in this environment.

Most plants need good-quality topsoil. Take some time to familiarise yourself with the various soil types, what they look like and how they feel. A good starting point is to visit a plant nursery or your local plant centre.

Building and landscape interfaces are often overlooked and uncoordinated. Reviewing interface details and levels around a building's perimeter is critical to ensure that awkward and unsightly mistakes do not reveal themselves during construction.

In this example, the lack of a bottom edge to the cladding, the open gap left between the wall and the soil and the poor quality of planting make this interface look like a mistake and appears unfinished.

A simple fix to this problem could be to plant evergreen species to cover this uncoordinated detail.

#83

People tend to take shortcuts and inadvertently damage any planting in the way. Desire lines should never be overlooked.

In some cases, mature evergreen plants may prevent people from cutting corners. However, planting beds should be maintained regularly to avoid gaps between the planting, which invite pedestrians to cut corners.

Although the best solution is to consider future desire lines in the layout of planting beds, installing a raised edge, a low railing or even a temporary fence will improve the situation. If the problem continues, consider changing the affected planted area with an informal path or stepping stones going through it.

This case study shows a series of empty planting beds under a north-facing colonnade. The scheme failed due to a lack of maintenance, irrigation and poor choice of plants.

Considering the planting beds' little exposure to rainfall, the project team should have allowed for automatic irrigation. Unfortunately, the team also failed to consider the appropriate plant species which survive in poor light conditions with a limited maintenance regime.

All in all, only a limited number of species can grow in these precarious conditions. And even the most resilient and adaptable species, such as ivies, struggle without care. Therefore, in this example, we recommend not planting anything at all.

In-ground tree uplighters set in planting often end up exposed because of soil compaction over time or lousy installation.

One could rely on maintenance to top up soil and/or mulch, but it may not offer the most reliable long-term solution.

At the design stage, consider more robust alternatives and ensure that particular luminaires do not impact local wildlife. For example, light fittings on stakes or bollards can provide more robust solutions in public spaces.

It is also important to consider cabling routes, luminaire driver locations and access for maintenance.

#86

#87

In this sh*tscape, aggregates were installed around an existing mature tree. One can see a large root poking out and the torn protective membrane. Always consider the relationship between a tree's roots and their growth, aggregate depths and surface levels to avoid future damage to the tree and potential trip hazards.

The aggregates weren't raked back into place, exposing the permeable membrane and leaving it susceptible to damage.

Loose aggregates will become a problem if maintenance isn't consistent or non-existent. Loose material tends to travel, especially if located under, or near, a heavily trafficked area. Even large, heavy aggregates, such as slate chippings, will drift over time under foot traffic.

During the design stage, it is crucial to inform the client team of a material's maintenance requirements and their long-term commitments. In most public open spaces, we recommend specifying a more robust surface if upkeep is uncertain or inconsistent over time.

Successful planting in raised planters can be challenging. It is crucial to consider drainage, irrigation and micro-climate and how it affects your choice of species.

In this instance, bare-rooted, medium-sized hedging plants are crammed into a very narrow planter in a windy location. A larger planter with container-grown plants suitable for exposed locations might have been more successful.

In nature, plants that grow in coastal or mountainous environments develop natural resistance to wind and dry soils. Therefore, we usually recommend planting short ground cover plants as these are more likely to survive strong, persistent winds.

#89

An unnecessary little brick planter became an ashtray by the roadside.

It is not always appropriate to add vegetation everywhere, just for the sake of it. Plants need space, appropriate soil volume, water and nutrients to grow, as well as the right level of care over time.

If the project team insist on putting plants in particularly challenging locations, temporary planters could be installed to test the resistance of plants against environmental conditions and maintenance regime.

Cor-ten is an excellent robust construction material widely used in urban landscape architecture projects due to its structural and aesthetical qualities. However, Cor-ten develops a thin layer of rust that can stain surrounding materials in the first year after exposure to the elements. Therefore, an off-site curing period is recommended, and a sealant should be applied and re-applied over time to avoid rust leaking onto the paving.

We recommend creating a shadow gap between any sensitive material and Cor-ten.

#91

Communication between the project team, especially when a contractor is setting out elements on site, is vital in ensuring your design is built as intended.

In this instance, the wall, the planter edge and the levels are completely out of sync. The edge should be aligned with the brick wall and come in at a 90-degree angle, the slot drain could have terminated at the corner, and the soil level should be higher.

Mitre joints tend to be vulnerable in external public environments. Ground settlement, thermal expansion and/or pedestrian and vehicular traffic put stress on these types of joints.

One could specify a corner unit or a simple ninety-degree joint for a more durable solution. If the stone is cut on site, remember to consider the finish of the exposed elevation.

In this example, a planter was installed on top of an existing ledge without any consideration for drainage. Excess water was allowed to drain directly onto the paving, creating stains caused by the calcium and magnesium in the soil.

This issue is much easier to prevent than to clean up. Integrated planters with well-designed outlets prevent water from seeping out of the planter's joints and draining onto the paving.

It is critical to provide access to any drainage outlets that might be covered by soil and planting. When planters are being retrofitted into an old scheme, existing gullies should be identified and incorporated into the design.

A perforated pipe, wrapped in geotextile, for rodding is essential for future access and maintenance.

#94

Looking at this case study, we see a damaged stone edge with no grout in the joint. In most cases, we do not recommend specifying mitre joints for street furniture in public open spaces.

These joints create thin, bevelled edges, making the material fragile and susceptible to chipping. Fluctuations in air temperature and humidity add further stress to the joint, as the material, in this case stone, will expand and contract.

Cladding panels are often proposed as a more cost-effective alternative to solid, thick blocks of stone. As a result, designers often specify mitre joints to make the elements look solid. However, maintenance costs will become more expensive over time than the original solution.

Sometimes, a rustic look is desired and can become a feature in your design. However, if the wood acts as a retaining edge, it is crucial to protect it from the wet soil / subgrade it retains. Installing a moisture-proof barrier will prevent water from soaking into the wood, avoiding fungal growth and eventually decay.

Often, temperature fluctuations and uncontrolled periods of excessive moisture in the air can result in timber beams cracking and twisting. Air-drying oak is a lengthy process and can be unpredictable, depending on the lengths needed for your design.

#96

We see this small mistake often with steel edging. If not correctly fixed together, the two pieces of steel will move independently from each other during construction and over time. When asphalt, concrete or aggregates are poured against these types of edges, they tend to twist or bend unevenly under the added pressure.

Always specify the connection type for the joint (welded or mechanical fixing), often shown as an option on manufacturers' websites. For a steel edge, we recommend specifying a hidden bolted connection with a clean finish on the visible side of the edge.

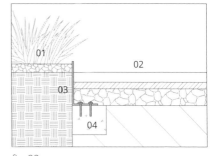

fig. 22

01 – planting
02 – paving slab
03 – steel or aluminium edge
04 – concrete foundation

Similar to case study #95, fixing steel edging firmly together is crucial, especially when it acts as a retaining edge against a flexible paving system. Since permeable paving on a flexible sand base is prone to movement, strong edging is necessary to keep the paving constrained.

In this example, the steel edge appears to be for aesthetics only, when it should actually serve as a retaining edge. Therefore, we recommend specifying bespoke corner pieces pre-bent to the desired angle, if cost allows. Installing a continuous steel edge creates a more robust detail that ensures the paving doesn't move over time.

#98

Bespoke details require additional thought and careful consideration to avoid unexpected issues on site.

In this example, the corner detail of a granite kerb with a curved profile wasn't fully considered.

A bespoke single-piece corner unit is the best option in this instance, as illustrated in fig. 05. Creating a mitre joint could be an alternative solution, but given its vulnerable location and sharp outward angle, it will likely get damaged over time.

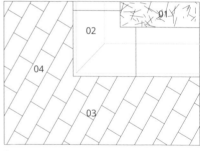

fig. 23

01 – planting
02 – solid corner unit
03 – paving blocks
04 – kerb

In this example, we see a Cor-ten steel edge next to a water feature for children. Unfortunately, the steel edge was left exposed and dangerously sharp. Therefore, a protective rubber strip was added to prevent any serious injury.

A more integrated solution would be to fold the steel inward to create a softer edge, as shown in the adjacent section.

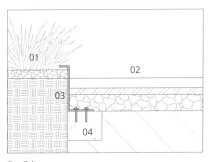

fig. 24

01 – planting
02 – paving
03 – steel edge with folded top edge
04 – concrete foundations

#100

Gaps and awkward cuts are created when the relationship between raised edges and the sloping ground isn't considered during the design stage.

Over sizing stone kerbs that extend below the surface is the best way to prevent these issues. Since built levels often differ from what was planned in a drawing, we recommend adding a little extra.

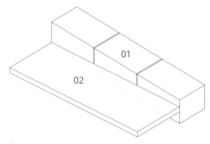

fig. 25

01 – stone kerb
02 – paved surface

© 2024 by jovis Verlag
An imprint of Walter de Gruyter GmbH, Berlin/Boston
Texts by kind permission of the authors.
Pictures by kind permission of the photographer.

Cover design: jovis Verlag
Photography: Vladimir Guculak
Proofreading: Bianca Murphy
Design and setting: Vladimir Guculak and Paul Bourel
Lithography: Bild1Druck, Berlin
Printed in the European Union.

Bibliographic information published by the Deutsche Nationalbibliothek
The Deutsche Nationalbibliothek lists this publication in the Deutsche
Nationalbibliografie; detailed bibliographic data are available on the Internet at
http://dnb.d-nb.de

jovis Verlag
Genthiner Straße 13
10785 Berlin

www.jovis.de

jovis books are available worldwide in select bookstores. Please contact your nearest
bookseller or visit www.jovis.de for information concerning your local distribution.

ISBN 978-3-98612-076-4 (softcover)
ISBN 978-3-98612-077-1 (e-book)